CW00521369

The New Air Fryer Cookbook

Easy Recipes to Fry, Bake, Grill and Roast. Enjoy the Crispness, Shed Weight and Reset Metabolism with Healthy and Affordable Recipes.

Ursula Mayert

Table of Contents

© Copyright 2020 by Ursula Mayert

- All rights reserved.

The following Book is reproduced below with the goal of providing information that is as accurate and reliable as possible. Regardless, purchasing this Book can be seen as consent to the fact that both the publisher and the author of this book are in no way experts on the topics discussed within and that any recommendations or suggestions that are made herein are for entertainment purposes only. Professionals should be consulted as needed prior to undertaking any of the action endorsed herein.

This declaration is deemed fair and valid by both the American Bar Association and the Committee of Publishers Association and is legally binding throughout the United States.

Furthermore, the transmission, duplication, or reproduction of any of the following work including specific information will be considered an illegal act irrespective of if it is done electronically or in print. This extends to creating a secondary or tertiary copy of the work or a recorded copy and is only allowed with the express written consent from the Publisher. All additional right reserved.

The information in the following pages is broadly considered a truthful and accurate account of facts and as such, any inattention, use, or misuse of the information in question by the reader will render any resulting actions solely under their purview. There are no scenarios in which the publisher or the original author of this work can be in any fashion deemed liable for any hardship or damages that may befall them after undertaking information described herein.

Additionally, the information in the following pages is intended only for informational purposes and should thus be thought of as universal. As befitting its nature, it is presented without assurance regarding its prolonged validity or interim quality. Trademarks that are mentioned are done without written consent and can in no way be considered an endorsement from the trademark holder.

Introduction

An air fryer is a relatively new kitchen appliance that has proven to be very popular among consumers. While there are many different varieties available, most air fryers share many common features. They all have heating elements that circulate hot air to cook the food. Most come with pre-programmed settings that assist users in preparing a wide variety of foods.

Air frying is a healthier style of cooking because it uses less oil than traditional deep frying methods. While it preserves the flavor and quality of the food, it reduces the amount of fat used in cooking. Air frying is a common method for "frying" foods that are primarily made with eggs and flour. These foods can be soft or crunchy to your preference by using this method.

How air fryers work

Air fryers use a blower to circulate hot air around food. The hot air heats the moisture on the food until it evaporates and creates steam. As steam builds up around the food, it creates pressure that pulls moisture from the surface of the food and pushes it away from the center, forming small bubbles. The bubbles creates a layer of air that surrounds the food and creates a crispy crust.

Choosing an air fryer

When choosing an air fryer, look for one that has good reviews for customer satisfaction. Start with the features you need, such as power, capacity size and accessories. Look for one that is easy to use. Some air fryers on the market have a built-in timer and adjustable temperature. Look for one with a funnel to catch grease, a basket that is dishwasher-safe and parts that are easy to clean.

How To Use An Air Fryer

For best results, preheat the air fryer at 400 F for 10 minutes. Preheating the air fryer allows it to reach the right temperature faster. In addition, preheating the air fryer is essential to ensure that your food won't burn.

How to cook stuff in an Air Fryer

If you don't have an air fryer yet, you can start playing with your ovens by throwing some frozen fries in there and cooking them until they are browned evenly. Depending on your oven, take a look at the temperature. You may need to increase or decrease the time.

What Foods Can You Cook In An Air Fryer?

Eggs: While you can cook eggs in an air fryer, we don't recommend it because you can't control the cooking time and temperature as precisely as with a traditional frying pan or skillet. It's much easier to get unevenly cooked eggs. You also can't toss in any sauces or seasonings and you won't get crispy, golden brown edges.

Frozen foods: Generally, frozen foods are best cooked in the conventional oven because they need to reach a certain temperature to be properly cooked. The air fryer is not capable of reaching temperatures that result in food being fully cooked.

Dehydrated Foods: Dehydrated foods require deep-frying, which is not something you can do with an air fryer. When it comes to cooking dehydrated foods, the air fryer is not the best option.

Vegetables: You can cook vegetables in an air fryer but you have to make sure that the air fryer is not set at a temperature that will burn them.

To ensure that your vegetables aren't overcooked, start the air fryer with the basket off, then toss in the veggies once the air has heated up and there are no more cold spots.

Make sure to stir the vegetables every few minutes. Cooking them in the basket is also an option, but they may stick together a little bit.

Fries: Frying fries in an air fryer is a good way to get crispy, golden-brown fries without adding lots of oil. Compared to conventional frying, air frying yields fewer calories.

To cook french fries in an air fryer, use a basket or a rack and pour in enough oil to come about halfway up the height of the fries. For best results, make sure the fries are frozen. Turn the air fryer onto 400 degrees and set it for 12 minutes. If you want them extra crispy, you can set it for 18 minutes, but they may burn a bit.

Benefits of an air fryer:

• It's one of the easiest ways to cook healthy foods. Used 4-5 times a week, it's a healthier option than frying with oil in your conventional oven or using canned foods.

• Air fryer meals are an easy way to serve tasty food that doesn't take up lots of space. Air fryers make it possible to cook three times as much food as you can in your microwave.

• Air fryers have a small footprint and you can store them away in a cabinet when not in use.

•They are versatile kitchen appliances. You can use them to cook food for lunch, dinner and snacks.

• Air fryers require little to no fussing in the kitchen. You can use them with the lid on, which means there's less washing up to do.

Fennel & Spinach Quiche

Basic Recipe

Preparation Time: 15 minutes

Cooking Time: 10 minutes

Servings: 5

Ingredients:

1   oz. fennel, chopped

2   1 cup spinach

3   eggs

4   ½ cup almond flour

5   1 teaspoon olive oil

6   1 tablespoon butter

7   1 teaspoon salt

8   ¼ cup heavy cream

9   1 teaspoon ground black pepper

Directions:

- Chop the spinach and combine it with the chopped fennel in a large bowl.
- Crack the egg in a separate bowl and whisk.
- Combine the whisked eggs with the almond flour, butter, salt, heavy cream, and ground black pepper.
- Whisk together to mix
- Preheat the air fryer to 360 F.
- Grease the air fryer basket tray with the olive oil.
- Add both mixtures.
- Cook the quiche for 18 minutes
- Let the quiche cool.
- Remove it from the air fryer and slice into servings.

Nutrition:

Calories 209

Fat 16.1

Carbs 7.4

Protein 8.3

Lemony Baby Potatoes

Basic Recipe

Preparation Time: 10 minutes

Cooking Time: 25 minutes

Servings: 6

Ingredients:

1. tablespoons olive oil
2. springs rosemary, chopped
3. tablespoons parsley, chopped
4. tablespoons oregano, chopped
5. Salt and black pepper to the taste
6. 1 tablespoon lemon rind, grated
7. garlic cloves, minced
8. tablespoons lemon juice
9. pounds baby potatoes

Directions:

- In a bowl, mix baby potatoes with oil, rosemary, parsley, oregano, salt, pepper, lemon rind, garlic and lemon juice, toss, transfer potatoes to your air fryer's basket and cook at 356 degrees F for 25 minutes
- Divide potatoes between plates and serve as a side dish.
- Enjoy!

Nutrition:

Calories 204

Fat 4

Carbs 17

Protein 6

Crispy Indian Wrap

Basic Recipe

Preparation Time: 20 minutes

Cooking Time: 8 minutes

Servings: 4

Ingredients:

- Cilantro Chutney
- 2¾ cups diced potato, cooked until tender
- teaspoons oil (coconut, sunflower, or safflower)
- large garlic cloves, minced or pressed
- 1½ tablespoons fresh lime juice
- 1½ teaspoons cumin powder
- 1 teaspoon onion granules
- 1 teaspoon coriander powder
- ½ teaspoon sea salt

- ½ teaspoon turmeric
- ¼ teaspoon cayenne powder
- large flour tortillas, preferably whole grain or sprouted
- 1 cup cooked garbanzo beans (canned are fine), rinsed and Dry out
- ½ cup finely chopped cabbage
- ¼ cup minced red onion or scallion
- Cooking oil spray (sunflower, safflower, or refined coconut)

Directions:

1   Make the Cilantro Chutney and set aside.

2   In a large bowl, mash the potatoes well, using a potato masher or large fork. Add the oil, garlic, lime, cumin, onion, coriander, salt, turmeric, and cayenne. Stir very well, until thoroughly combined. Set aside.

3   Lay the tortillas out flat on the counter. In the middle of each, evenly distribute the potato filling. Add some of the garbanzo beans, cabbage, and red onion to each, on top of the potatoes.

4   Spray the air fryer basket with oil and set aside. Enclose the Indian wraps by folding the bottom of the tortillas up and over the filling, then folding the sides in—and finally rolling the bottom up to form, essentially, an enclosed burrito.

5   Place the wraps in the air fryer basket, seam side down. They can touch each other a little bit, but if they're too crowded, you'll need to cook them in batches. Fry for 5 minutes Spray with oil again, flip over, and cook an additional 2 or 3 minutes, until nicely browned and crisp. Serve topped with the Cilantro Chutney.

Nutrition:

Calories 288

Fat 7g

Carbs 50g

Protein 9g

Easy Peasy Pizza

Basic Recipe

Preparation Time: 5 minutes

Cooking Time: 10 minutes

Servings: 4

Ingredients:

- Cooking oil spray (coconut, sunflower, or safflower)
- 1 flour tortilla, preferably sprouted or whole grain
- ¼ cup vegan pizza or marinara sauce
- ⅓Cup grated vegan mozzarella cheese or Cheesy Sauce
- Toppings of your choice

Directions:

1   Spray the air fryer basket with oil. Place the tortilla in the air fryer basket. If the tortilla is a little bigger than the base, no problem! Simply fold the edges up a bit to form a semblance of a "crust."

2   Pour the sauce in the center, and evenly distribute it around the tortilla "crust" (I like to use the back of a spoon for this purpose).

3   Sprinkle evenly with vegan cheese, and add your toppings. Bake it for 9 minutes, or until nicely browned. Remove carefully, cut into four pieces, and enjoy.

Nutrition:

Calories 210

Fat 6g

Carbs 33g

Protein 5g

Eggplant Parmigiana

Basic Recipe

Preparation Time: 15 minutes

Cooking Time: 40 minutes

Servings: 4

Ingredients:

1. 1 medium eggplant (about 1 pound), sliced into ½-inch-thick rounds
2. tablespoons tamari or shoyu
3. tablespoons nondairy milk, plain and unsweetened
4. 1 cup chickpea flour (see Substitution Tip)
5. 1 tablespoon dried basil
6. 1 tablespoon dried oregano
7. teaspoons garlic granules
8. teaspoons onion granules
9. ½ teaspoon sea salt
10. ½ teaspoons freshly ground black pepper
11. Cooking oil spray (sunflower, safflower, or refined coconut)
12. Vegan marinara sauce (your choice)
13. Shredded vegan cheese (preferably mozzarella; see Ingredient Tip)

Directions:

- Place the eggplant slices in a large bowl, and pour the tamari and milk over the top. Turn the pieces over to coat them as evenly as possible with the liquids. Set aside.
- Make the coating: In a medium bowl, combine the flour, basil, oregano, garlic, onion, salt, and pepper and stir well. Set aside.
- Spray the air fryer basket with oil and set aside.
- Stir the eggplant slices again and transfer them to a plate (stacking is fine). Do not discard the liquid in the bowl.
- Bread the eggplant by tossing an eggplant round in the flour mixture. Then, dip in the liquid again. Double up on the coating by placing the eggplant again in the flour mixture, making sure that all sides are nicely breaded. Place in the air fryer basket.
- Repeat with enough eggplant rounds to make a (mostly) single layer in the air fryer basket. (You'll need to cook it in batches, so that you don't have too much overlap and it cooks perfectly.)

- Spray the tops of the eggplant with enough oil so that you no longer see dry patches in the coating. Fry for 8 minutes. Remove the air fryer basket and spray the tops again. Turn each piece over, again taking care not to overlap the rounds too much. Spray the tops with oil, again making sure that no dry patches remain. Fry for another 8 minutes, or until nicely browned and crisp.
- Repeat steps 5 to 7 one more time, or until all of the eggplant is crisp and browned.
- Finally, place half of the eggplant in a 6-inch round, 2-inch deep baking pan and top with marinara sauce and a sprinkle of vegan cheese. Fry for 3 minutes, or until the sauce is hot and cheese is melted (be careful not to overcook, or the eggplant edges will burn). Serve immediately, plain or over pasta. Otherwise, you can store the eggplant in the fridge for several days and then make a fresh batch whenever the mood strikes by repeating this step!

Nutrition:

Calories 217

Fat 9g

Carbs 38g

Protein 9g

Luscious Lazy Lasagna

Basic Recipe

Preparation Time: 15 minutes

Cooking Time: 15 minutes

Servings: 4

Ingredients:

1. ounces lasagna noodles, preferably bean-based, but any kind will do
2. 1 tablespoon extra-virgin olive oil
3. cups crumbled extra-firm tofu, Dry out and water squeezed out
4. cups loosely packed fresh spinach
5. tablespoons nutritional yeast
6. tablespoons fresh lemon juice
7. 1 teaspoon onion granules
8. 1 teaspoon sea salt
9. ⅛ Teaspoon freshly ground black pepper
10. large garlic cloves, minced or pressed
11. cups vegan pasta sauce, your choice
12. ½ cup shredded vegan cheese (preferably mozzarella)

Directions:

- Cook the noodles until a little firmer than al dente (they'll get a little softer after you air-fry them in the lasagna). Dry out and set aside.

- While the noodles are cooking, make the filling. In a large pan over medium-high heat, add the olive oil, tofu, and spinach. Stir-fry for a minute, then add the nutritional yeast, lemon juice, onion, salt, pepper, and garlic. Stir well and cook just until the spinach is nicely wilted. Remove from heat.
- To make half a batch (one 6-inch round, 2-inch deep baking pan) of lasagna: Spread a thin layer of pasta sauce in the baking pan. Layer 2 or 3 lasagna noodles on top of the sauce. Top with a little more sauce and some of the tofu mixture. Place another 2 or 3 noodles on top, and add another layer of sauce and then another layer of tofu. Finish with a layer of noodles, and then a final layer of sauce. Sprinkle about half of the vegan cheese on top (omit if you prefer; see the Ingredient Tip from the Eggplant Parmigiana). Place the pan in the air fryer and Bake it for 15 minutes, or until the noodles are browning around the edges and the cheese is melted. Cut and serve.

Nutrition:

Calories 317

Fat 8g

Carbs 46g

Protein 20g

Pasta with Creamy Cauliflower Sauce

Basic Recipe

Preparation Time: 10 minutes

Cooking Time: 20 minutes

Servings: 4

Ingredients:

1. cups cauliflower florets
2. Cooking oil spray (sunflower,
3. Safflower, or refined coconut)
4. 1 medium onion, chopped
5. ounces pasta, your choice (about 4 cups cooked; use gluten-free pasta if desired)
6. Fresh chives or scallion tops, for garnish
7. ½ cup raw cashew pieces (see Ingredient Tip)

8   1½ cups water

9   1 tablespoon nutritional yeast

10   large garlic cloves, peeled

11   tablespoons fresh lemon juice

12   1½ teaspoons sea salt

13   ¼ teaspoons freshly ground black pepper

Directions:

- Place the cauliflower in the air fryer basket, sprits the tops with oil spray, and roast for 8 minutes Remove the air fryer basket, stir, and add the onion. Sprits with oil again and roast for another 10 minutes, or until the cauliflower is browned and the onions are tender.

- While the vegetables are roasting in the air fryer, cook the pasta according to the package directions and mince the chives or scallions. Set aside.

- In a blender jar, place the roasted cauliflower and onions along with the cashews, water, nutritional yeast, garlic, lemon, salt, and pepper. Blend well, until very smooth and creamy. Serve a generous portion of the sauce on top of the warm pasta, and top with the minced chives or scallions. The sauce will store, refrigerated in an airtight container, for about a week.

Nutrition:

Calories 341

Fat 9g

Carbs 51g

Protein 14g

Lemony Lentils with "Fried" Onions

Basic Recipe

Preparation Time: 10 minutes

Cooking Time: 30 minutes

Servings: 4

Ingredients:

1. 1 cup red lentils
2. cups water
3. Cooking oil spray (coconut, sunflower, or safflower)
4. 1 medium-size onion, peeled and cut into ¼-inch-thick rings
5. Sea salt
6. ½ cup kale, stems removed, thinly sliced
7. large garlic cloves, pressed or minced
8. tablespoons fresh lemon juice
9. teaspoons nutritional yeast
10. 1 teaspoon sea salt
11. 1 teaspoon lemon zest (see Ingredient Tip)
12. ¾ teaspoons freshly ground black pepper

Directions:

- In a medium-large pot, bring the lentils and water to a boil over medium-high heat.

- Reduce the heat to low and simmer, uncovered, for about 30 minutes (or until the lentils have dissolved completely), making sure to stir every 5 minutes or so as they cook (so that the lentils don't stick to the bottom of the pot).
- While the lentils are cooking, get the rest of your dish together.
- Spray the air fryer basket with oil and place the onion rings inside, separating them as much as possible. Spray them with the oil and sprinkle with a little salt. Fry for 5 minutes.
- Remove the air fryer basket, shake or stir, spray again with oil, and fry for another 5 minutes.
- (Note: You're aiming for all of the onion slices to be crisp and well browned, so if some of the pieces begin to do that, transfer them from the air fryer basket to a plate.)
- Remove the air fryer basket, spray the onions again with oil, and fry for a final 5 minutes or until all the pieces are crisp and browned.
- To finish the lentils: Add the kale to the hot lentils, and stir very well, as the heat from the lentils will steam the thinly sliced greens.
- Stir in the garlic, lemon juice, nutritional yeast, salt, zest, and pepper.

- Stir very well and then distribute evenly in bowls. Top with the crisp onion rings and serve.

Nutrition:

Calories 220

Fat 1g

Carbs 39g

Protein 15g

Our Daily Bean

Basic Recipe

Preparation Time: 5 minutes

Cooking Time: 10 minutes

Servings: 4

Ingredients:

1. 1 (15-ounce) can pinto beans, Dry out
2. ¼ cup tomato sauce
3. tablespoons nutritional yeast
4. large garlic cloves, pressed or minced
5. ½ teaspoon dried oregano
6. ½ teaspoon cumin
7. ¼ teaspoon sea salt
8. ⅛ Teaspoon freshly ground black pepper
9. Cooking oil spray (sunflower, safflower, or refined coconut)

Directions:

- In a medium bowl, stir together the beans, tomato sauce, nutritional yeast, garlic, oregano, cumin, salt, and pepper until well combined.

- Spray the 6-inch round, 2-inch deep baking pan with oil and pour the bean mixture into it. Bake it for 4 minutes Remove, stir well, and Bake it for another 4 minutes, or until the mixture has thickened and is heated through. It will most likely form a little crust on top and be lightly browned in spots. Serve hot. This will keep, refrigerated in an airtight container, for up to a week.

Nutrition:

Calories 284

Fat 4g

Carbs 47g

Protein 20g

Taco Salad with Creamy Lime Sauce

Basic Recipe

Preparation Time: 10 minutes

Cooking Time: 10 minutes

Servings: 4

Ingredients:

For The Sauce

1. 1 (12.3-ounce) package of silken-firm tofu
2. ¼ cup plus 1 tablespoon fresh lime juice
3. Zest of 1 large lime (1 teaspoon)
4. 1½ tablespoons coconut sugar
5. large garlic cloves, peeled
6. 1 teaspoon sea salt
7. ½ teaspoon ground chipotle powder

For The Salad

- cups romaine lettuce, chopped (1 large head)
- 1 (15-ounce) can vegan refried beans (or whole pinto or black beans if you prefer)
- 1 cup chopped red cabbage
- medium tomatoes, chopped
- ½ cup chopped cilantro
- ¼ cup minced scallions
- Double batch of garlic lime tortilla chips

Directions:

1. To Make the Sauce
2. Dry out the tofu (pour off any liquid) and place in a blender.
3. Add the lime juice and zest, coconut sugar, garlic, salt, and chipotle powder. Blend until very smooth. Set aside.
4. To Make the Salad
5. Distribute the lettuce equally into three big bowls.
6. In a small pan over medium heat, warm the beans, stirring often, until hot (this should take less than a minute). Place on top of the lettuce.
7. Top the beans with the cabbage, tomatoes, cilantro, and scallions.
8. Drizzle with generously with the Creamy Lime Sauce and serve with the double batch of air-fried chips. Enjoy immediately.

Nutrition:

Calories 422

Fat 7g

Carbs 71g

Protein 22g

BBQ Jackfruit Nachos

Basic Recipe

Preparation Time: 30 minutes

Cooking Time: 20 minutes

Servings: 4

Ingredients:

- 1 (20-ounce) can jackfruit, dry out
- ⅓cup prepared vegan bbq sauce
- ¼ cup water
- tablespoons tamari or shoyu
- 1 tablespoon fresh lemon juice
- large garlic cloves, pressed or minced
- 1 teaspoon onion granules
- ⅛ Teaspoon cayenne powder
- ⅛ Teaspoon liquid smoke
- Double batch garlic lime tortilla chips
- 2½ cups prepared cheesy sauce
- medium-size tomatoes, chopped
- ¾ cup guacamole of your choice
- ¾ cup chopped cilantro
- ½ cup minced red onion
- 1 jalapeño, seeds removed and thinly sliced (optional)

Directions:

1. In a large skillet over high heat, place the jackfruit, BBQ sauce, water, tamari, lemon juice, garlic, onion granules, cayenne, and liquid smoke. Stir well and break up the jackfruit a bit with a spatula.

2. Once the mixture boils, reduce the heat to low. Continue to cook, stirring often (and breaking up the jackfruit as you stir), for about 20 minutes, or until all of the liquid has been absorbed. Remove from the heat and set aside.

3. Assemble the nachos: Distribute the chips onto three plates, and then top evenly with the jackfruit mixture, warmed Cheesy Sauce, tomatoes, guacamole, cilantro, onion, and jalapeño (if using). Enjoy immediately, because soggy chips are tragic.

Nutrition:

Calories 661

Fat 15g

Carbs 124g

Protein 22g

10-Minute Chimichanga

Basic Recipe

Preparation Time: 5 minutes

Cooking Time: 10 minutes

Servings: 4

Ingredients:

- 1 whole-grain tortilla
- ½ cup vegan refried beans
- ¼ cup grated vegan cheese (optional)
- Cooking oil spray (sunflower, safflower, or refined coconut)
- ½ cup fresh salsa (or Green Chili Sauce)
- cups chopped romaine lettuce (about ½ head)
- Guacamole (optional)
- Chopped cilantro (optional)
- Cheesy Sauce (optional)

Directions:

1   Lay the tortilla on a flat surface and place the beans in the center. Top with the cheese, if using. Wrap the bottom up over the filling, and then fold in the sides. Then roll it all up so as to enclose the beans inside the tortilla (you're making an enclosed burrito here).

2   Spray the air fryer basket with oil, place the tortilla wrap inside the basket, seam-side down, and spray the top of the chimichanga with oil. Fry for 5 minutes Spray the top (and sides) again with oil, flip over, and spray the other side with oil. Fry for an additional 2 or 3 minutes, until nicely browned and crisp.

3   Transfer to a plate. Top with the salsa, lettuce, guacamole, cilantro, and/or Cheesy Sauce, if using. Serve immediately.

Nutrition:

Calories 317

Fat 6g

Carbs 55g

Protein 13g

Mexican Stuffed Potatoes

Intermediate Recipe

Preparation Time: 15 minutes

Cooking Time: 40 minutes

Servings: 4

Ingredients:

- large potatoes, any variety (I like Yukon Gold or russets for this dish; see Cooking Tip)
- Cooking oil spray (sunflower, safflower, or refined coconut)
- 1½ cups Cheesy Sauce
- 1 cup black or pinto beans (canned beans are fine; be sure to Dry out and rinse)
- medium tomatoes, chopped
- 1 scallion, finely chopped
- ⅓ Cup finely chopped cilantro
- 1 jalapeño, finely sliced or minced (optional)
- 1 avocado, diced (optional)

Directions:

1   Scrub the potatoes, prick with a fork, and spray the outsides with oil. Place in the air fryer (leaving room in between so the air can circulate) and Bake it for 30 minutes

2   While the potatoes are cooking, prepare the Cheesy Sauce and additional items. Set aside.

3   Check the potatoes at the 30-minute mark by poking a fork into them. If they're very tender, they're done. If not, continue to cook until a fork inserted proves them to be well-done. (As potato sizes vary, so will your cook time—the average cook time is usually about 40 minutes)

4   When the potatoes are getting very close to being tender, warm the Cheesy Sauce and the beans in separate pans.

5   To assemble: Plate the potatoes and cut them across the top. Then, pry them open with a fork—just enough to get all the goodies in there. Top each potato with the Cheesy Sauce, beans, tomatoes, scallions, cilantro, and jalapeño and avocado, if using. Enjoy immediately.

Nutrition:

Calories 420

Fat 5g

Carbs 80g

Fiber 17g

Protein 15g

Kids' Taquitos

Basic Recipe

Preparation Time: 5 minutes

Cooking Time: 10 minutes

Servings: 4

Ingredients:

- corn tortillas
- Cooking oil spray (coconut, sunflower, or safflower)
- 1 (15-ounce) can vegan refried beans
- 1 cup shredded vegan cheese
- Guacamole (optional)
- Cheesy Sauce (optional)
- Vegan sour cream (optional)
- Fresh salsa (optional)

Directions:

1   Warm the tortillas (so they don't break): Run them under water for a second, and then place in an oil-sprayed air fryer basket (stacking them is fine). Fry for 1 minute.

2   Remove to a flat surface, laying them out individually. Place an equal amount of the beans in a line down the center of each tortilla. Top with the vegan cheese.

3   Roll the tortilla sides up over the filling and place seam-side down in the air fryer basket (this will help them seal so the tortillas don't fly open). Add just enough to fill the basket without them touching too much (you may need to do another batch, depending on the size of your air fryer basket).

4   Spray the tops with oil. Fry for 7 minutes, or until the tortillas are golden-brown and lightly crisp. Serve immediately with your preferred toppings.

Nutrition:

Calories 286

Fat 9g

Carbs 44g

Protein 9g

Immune-Boosting Grilled Cheese Sandwich

Basic Recipe
Preparation Time: 5 minutes
Cooking Time: 15 minutes
Servings: 4
Ingredients:

- slices sprouted whole-grain bread (or substitute a gluten-free bread)
- 1 teaspoon vegan margarine or neutral-flavored oil (sunflower, safflower, or refined coconut)
- slices vegan cheese (Violife cheddar or Chao creamy original) or Cheesy Sauce
- 1 teaspoon mellow white miso
- 1 medium-large garlic clove, pressed or finely minced
- tablespoons fermented vegetables, kimchi, or sauerkraut
- Romaine or green leaf lettuce

Directions:

1   Spread the outsides of the bread with the vegan margarine. Place the sliced cheese inside and close the sandwich back up again (buttered sides facing out). Place the sandwich in the air fryer basket and fry for 6 minutes Flip over and fry for another 6 minutes, or until nicely browned and crisp on the outside.

2   Transfer to a plate. Open the sandwich and evenly
    spread the miso and garlic clove over the inside of one
    of the bread slices. Top with the fermented vegetables
    and lettuce, close the sandwich back up, cut in half, and
    serve immediately.

Nutrition:

Calories 288

Fat 13g

Carbs 34g

Protein 8g

Tamale Pie with Cilantro Lime Cornmeal Crust

Basic Recipe

Preparation Time: 25 minutes

Cooking Time: 20 minutes

Servings: 4

Ingredients:

For the filling

- 1 medium zucchini, diced (1¼ cups)
- teaspoons neutral-flavored oil (sunflower, safflower, or refined coconut)
- 1 cup cooked pinto beans, Dry out
- 1 cup canned diced tomatoes (unsalted) with juice
- large garlic cloves, minced or pressed
- 1 tablespoon chickpea flour
- 1 teaspoon dried oregano
- 1 teaspoon onion granules
- ½ teaspoon salt
- ½ teaspoon crushed red chili flakes
- Cooking oil spray (sunflower, safflower, or refined coconut)

For the crust

- ½ cup yellow cornmeal, finely ground
- 1½ cups water

- ½ teaspoon salt
- 1 teaspoon nutritional yeast
- 1 teaspoon neutral-flavored oil (sunflower, safflower, or refined coconut)
- tablespoons finely chopped cilantro
- ½ teaspoon lime zest

Directions:

1. To make the filling
2. In a large skillet set to medium-high heat, sauté the zucchini and oil for 3 minutes or until the zucchini begins to brown.
3. Add the beans, tomatoes, garlic, flour, oregano, onion, salt, and chili flakes to the mixture. Cook it over medium heat, stirring often, for 5 minutes, or until the mixture is thickened and no liquid remains. Remove from the heat.
4. Spray a 6-inch round, 2-inch deep baking pan with oil and place the mixture in the bottom. Smooth out the top and set aside.
5. To make the crust

6   In a medium pot over high heat, place the cornmeal, water, and salt. Whisk constantly as you bring the mixture to a boil. Once it boils, reduce the heat to very low. Add the nutritional yeast and oil and continue to cook, stirring very often, for 10 minutes or until the mixture is very thick and hard to whisk. Remove from the heat.

7   Stir the cilantro and lime zest into the cornmeal mixture until thoroughly combined. Using a rubber spatula, gently spread it evenly onto the filling in the baking pan to form a smooth crust topping. Place in the air fryer basket and Bake it for 20 minutes, or until the top is golden-brown. Let it cool for 5 to 10 minutes, then cut and serve.

Nutrition:

Calories 165

Fat 5g

Carbs 26g

Protein 6g

Herbed Eggplant

Basic Recipe

Preparation Time: 15 minutes

Cooking Time: 15 minutes

Servings: 2

Ingredients

- ½ teaspoon dried marjoram, crushed
- ½ teaspoon dried oregano, crushed
- ½ teaspoon dried thyme, crushed
- ½ teaspoon garlic powder
- Salt and ground black pepper, as required
- 1 large eggplant, cubed

- Olive oil cooking spray

Directions:

1   Set the temperature of air fryer to 390 degrees F. Grease an air fryer basket.

2   In a small bowl, mix well herbs, garlic powder, salt, and black pepper.

3   Spray the eggplant cubes evenly with cooking spray and then, rub with the herbs mixture.

4   Arrange eggplant cubes into the prepared air fryer basket in a single layer.

5   Air fry for about 6 minutes

6   Flip and spray the eggplant cubes with cooking spray.

7   Air fry for another 6 minutes

8   Flip and again, spray the eggplant cubes with cooking spray.

9   Air fry for 2-3 more minutes

10 Remove from air fryer and transfer the eggplant cubes onto serving plates.

11 Serve hot.

Nutrition:

Calories 62

Carbs 14.5g

Protein 2.4g

Fat 0.5g

Spices Stuffed Eggplants

Basic Recipe

Preparation Time: 15 minutes

Cooking Time: 12 minutes

Servings: 4

Ingredients

- teaspoons olive oil, divided
- ¾ tablespoon dry mango powder
- ¾ tablespoon ground coriander
- ½ teaspoon ground cumin
- ½ teaspoon ground turmeric
- ½ teaspoon garlic powder
- Salt, to taste
- baby eggplants

Directions:

1 In a small bowl, mix together one teaspoon of oil, and spices.

2 From the bottom of each eggplant, make 2 slits, leaving the stems intact.

3 With a small spoon, fill each slit of eggplants with spice mixture.

4 Now, brush the outer side of each eggplant with remaining oil.

5 Set the temperature of air fryer to 369 degrees F. Grease an air fryer basket.

6 Arrange eggplants into the prepared air fryer basket in a single layer.

7 Air fry for about 8-12 minutes

8 Remove from air fryer and transfer the eggplants onto serving plates.

9 Serve hot.

Nutrition:

Calories 317

Carbs 65g

Protein 10.9g

Fat 6.7g

Salsa Stuffed Eggplants

Basic Recipe

Preparation Time: 15 minutes

Cooking Time: 25 minutes

Servings: 2

Ingredients

- 1 large eggplant
- teaspoons olive oil, divided
- teaspoons fresh lemon juice, divided
- 8 cherry tomatoes, quartered
- 3 tablespoons tomato salsa
- ½ tablespoon fresh parsley
- Salt and ground black pepper, as required

Directions:

1 Set the temperature of air fryer to 390 degrees F. Grease an air fryer basket.

2 Place eggplant into the prepared air fryer basket.

3 Air fry for about 15 minutes

4 Remove from air fryer and cut the eggplant in half lengthwise.

5 Drizzle with the eggplant halves evenly with one teaspoon of oil.

6 Now, set the temperature of air fryer to 355 degrees F. Grease the air fryer basket.

7   Arrange eggplant into the prepared air fryer basket, cut-side up.

8   Air fry for another 10 minutes

9   Remove eggplant from the air fryer and set aside for about 5 minutes

10 Carefully, scoop out the flesh, leaving about ¼-inch away from edges.

11 Drizzle with the eggplant halves with one teaspoon of lemon juice.

12 Transfer the eggplant flesh into a bowl.

13 Add the tomatoes, salsa, parsley, salt, black pepper, remaining oil, and lemon juice and mix well.

14 Stuff the eggplant haves with salsa mixture and serve.

Nutrition:

Calories 192

Carbs 33.8g

Protein 6.9g

Fat 6.1g

Sesame Seeds Bok Choy

Basic Recipe

Preparation Time: 10 minutes

Cooking Time: 6 minutes

Servings: 4

Ingredients

- bunches baby bok choy, bottoms removed and leaves separated
- Olive oil cooking spray
- 1 teaspoon garlic powder

- 1 teaspoon sesame seeds

Directions:

1   Set the temperature of air fryer to 325 degrees F.
2   Arrange bok choy leaves into the air fryer basket in a single layer.
3   Spray with the cooking spray and sprinkle with garlic powder.
4   Air fry for about 5-6 minutes, shaking after every 2 minutes
5   Remove from air fryer and transfer the bok choy onto serving plates.
6   Garnish with sesame seeds and serve hot.

Nutrition:

Calories 26

Carbs 4g

Protein 2.5g

Fat 0.7g

Basil Tomatoes

Basic Recipe

Preparation Time: 10 minutes

Cooking Time: 10 minutes

Servings: 2

Ingredients:

- tomatoes, halved
- Olive oil cooking spray
- Salt and ground black pepper, as required
- 1 tablespoon fresh basil, chopped

Directions:

1 Set the temperature of air fryer to 320 degrees F. Grease an air fryer basket.
2 Spray the tomato halves evenly with cooking spray and sprinkle with salt, black pepper and basil.
3 Arrange tomato halves into the prepared air fryer basket, cut sides up.
4 Air-fry it for about 10 minutes or until desired doneness.
5 Remove from air fryer and transfer the tomatoes onto serving plates.
6 Serve warm.

Nutrition:

Calories 22

Carbs 4.8g

Protein 1.1g

Fat 4.8g

Overloaded Tomatoes

Basic Recipe

Preparation Time: 15 minutes

Cooking Time: 22 minutes

Servings: 4

Ingredients:

- tomatoes
- 1 teaspoon olive oil
- 1 carrot, peeled and finely chopped
- 1 onion, chopped
- 1 cup frozen peas, thawed
- 1 garlic clove, minced
- cups cold cooked rice

- 1 tablespoon soy sauce

Directions:

1. Cut the top of each tomato and scoop out pulp and seeds. In a skillet, heat oil over low heat and sauté the carrot, onion, garlic, and peas for about 2 minutes

2. Stir in the soy sauce and rice and remove from heat. Set the temperature of air fryer to 355 degrees F. Grease an air fryer basket.

3. Stuff each tomato with the rice mixture.

4. Arrange tomatoes into the prepared air fryer basket.

5. Air fry for about 20 minutes

6. Remove from air fryer and transfer the tomatoes onto a serving platter.

7. Set aside to cool slightly.

8. Serve warm.

Nutrition:

Calories 421

Carbs 89.1g

Protein 10.5g

Fat 2.2g

Sweet & Spicy Cauliflower

Basic Recipe

Preparation Time: 15 minutes

Cooking Time: 30 minutes

Servings: 4

Ingredients

- 1 head cauliflower, cut into florets
- ¾ cup onion, thinly sliced
- garlic cloves, finely sliced
- 1½ tablespoons soy sauce
- 1 tablespoon hot sauce
- 1 tablespoon rice vinegar
- 1 teaspoon coconut sugar
- Pinch of red pepper flakes
- Ground black pepper, as required
- scallions, chopped

Directions:

1 Set the temperature of air fryer to 350 degrees F. Grease an air fryer pan. Arrange cauliflower florets into the prepared air fryer pan in a single layer.

2 Air fry for about 10 minutes

3 Remove from air fryer and stir in the onions.

4 Air fry for another 10 minutes

5 Remove from air fryer and stir in the garlic.

6   Air fry for 5 more minutes

7   Meanwhile, in a bowl, mix well soy sauce, hot sauce, vinegar, coconut sugar, red pepper flakes, and black pepper.

8   Remove from the air fryer and stir in the sauce mixture.

9   Air fry for about 5 minutes

10 Remove from air fryer and transfer the cauliflower mixture onto serving plates. Garnish with scallions and serve.

Nutrition:

Calories 72

Carbs 13.8g

Protein 3.6g

Fat 0.2g

Herbed Potatoes

Basic Recipe

Preparation Time: 10 minutes

Cooking Time: 16 minutes

Servings: 4

Ingredients

1 small potatoes, chopped

2 tablespoons olive oil

3 teaspoons mixed dried herbs

4 Salt and ground black pepper, as required

5 tablespoons fresh parsley, chopped

Directions:

- Set the temperature of air fryer to 356 degrees F. Grease an air fryer basket.
- In a large bowl, add the potatoes, oil, herbs, salt and black pepper and toss to coat well. Arrange the chopped potatoes into the prepared air fryer basket in a single layer.
- Air fry it for about 16 minutes, tossing once halfway through.
- Remove from air fryer and transfer the potatoes onto serving plates. Garnish with parsley and serve.

Nutrition:

Calories 268

Carbs 40.4g

Protein 4.4g

Fat 10.8g

Spicy Potatoes

Basic Recipe

Preparation Time: 10 minutes

Cooking Time: 20 minutes

Servings: 6

Ingredients

1. 1¾ pounds waxy potatoes, peeled and cubed
2. 1 tablespoon olive oil
3. ½ teaspoon ground cumin
4. ½ teaspoon ground coriander
5. ½ teaspoon paprika
6. Salt and freshly ground black pepper, as required

Directions:

- In a large bowl of water, add the potatoes and set aside for about 30 minutes
- Dry out the potatoes completely and dry with paper towels.
- In a bowl, add the potatoes, oil, and spices and toss to coat well.
- Set the temperature of air fryer to 355 degrees F. Grease an air fryer basket.
- Arrange potato pieces into the prepared air fryer basket in a single layer.
- Air fry for about 20 minutes

- Remove from air fryer and transfer the potato pieces onto serving plates.
- Serve hot.

Nutrition:

Calories 113

Fat 2.5g

Carbs 21g

Protein 2.3g

Crispy Kale Chips

Basic Recipe

Preparation Time: 5 minutes

Cooking Time: 7 minutes

Servings: 3

Ingredients:

3 cups kale leaves, stems removed

1 tablespoon olive oil

Salt and pepper, to taste

Directions:

- In a bowl, combine all of the ingredients. Toss to coat the kale leaves with oil, salt, and pepper.
- Arrange the kale leaves on the double layer rack and insert inside the air fryer.
- Close the air fryer and cook for 7 minutes at 3700F.
- Allow to cool before serving.

Nutrition:

Calories 48

Carbs 1.4g

Protein 0.7g

Fat 4.8g

Grilled Buffalo Cauliflower

Basic Recipe

Preparation Time: 5 minutes

Cooking Time: 5 minutes

Servings: 1

Ingredients:

- 1 cup cauliflower florets
- Cooking oil spray
- Salt and pepper, to taste
- ½ cup buffalo sauce

Directions

- Place the cauliflower florets in a bowl and spray with cooking oil. Season it with salt and pepper.
- Toss to coat.
- Place the grill pan in the air fryer and add the cauliflower florets.
- Close the lid and cook for 5 minutes at 390oF.
- Once cooked, place in a bowl and pour the buffalo sauce over the top. Toss to coat.

Nutrition:

Calories 25

Fat 0.1g

Carbs 5.3g

Protein 2g

Faux Fried Pickles

Basic Recipe

Preparation Time: 5 minutes

Cooking Time: 5 minutes

Servings: 2

Ingredients:

1   1 cup pickle slices

2   1 egg, beaten

3   ½ cup grated Parmesan cheese

4   ½ cup almond flour

5   ¼ cup pork rinds, crushed

6   Salt and pepper, to taste

Directions

- Place the pickles in a bowl and pour the beaten egg over the top. Allow to soak.

- In another dish or bowl, combine the Parmesan cheese, almond flour, pork rinds, salt, and pepper.

- Dredge the pickles in the Parmesan cheese mixture and place on the double layer rack.

- Place the rack with the pickles inside of the air fryer.

- Close the lid and cook for 5 minutes at 390oF.

Nutrition:

Calories 664

Carbs 17.9g

Protein 42g

Fat 49.9g

Greatest Green Beans

Basic Recipe

Preparation Time: 5 minutes

Cooking Time: 5 minutes

Servings: 2

Ingredients:

1   1 cup green beans, trimmed

2   ½ teaspoon oil

3   Salt and pepper, to taste

Directions

- Place the green beans in a bowl and add in oil, salt, and pepper.
- Toss to coat the beans.
- Place the grill pan in the air fryer and add the green beans in a single layer.
- Close the lid and cook for 5 minutes at 3900F.

Nutrition

Calories 54

Fat 2.5g

Carbs 7.7g

Protein 2g

Summer Grilled Corn

Basic Recipe

Preparation Time: 5 minutes

Cooking Time: 10 minutes

Servings: 2

Ingredients:

1. corns on the cob cut into halves widthwise
2. ½ teaspoon oil
3. Salt and pepper, to taste

Directions:

- Brush the corn cobs with oil and season with salt and pepper.
- Place the grill pan accessory into the air fryer.
- Place the corn cobs on the grill pan.
- Close the lid and cook for 3 minutes at 3900F.
- Open the air fryer and turn the corn cobs.
- Cook for another 3 minutes at the same temperature.

Nutrition:

Calories 173

Carbs 29g

Protein 4.5 g

Fat 4.5g

Cheesy Bean Bake

Basic Recipe

Preparation Time: 5 minutes

Cooking Time: 55 minutes

Servings: 6

Ingredients:

1. tbsp. extra-virgin olive oil
2. ½ tsp. black pepper
3. 1 1/3 cups mozzarella coarsely grated
4. 1 1/2 tsp. garlic, sliced
5. tbsp. tomato paste
6. 1 1/3 cups dried beans
7. ½ tsp. kosher salt

Directions:

- Pressure Cook beans with 4 cups water on High for 25 minutes. Sauté beans with oil.
- Add garlic and cook for 1 minute. Add beans, tomato paste, water, a pinch of salt and pepper.
- Top with cheese.
- Press Broil for 7 minutes with Air Fryer Lid. Serve with toasted bread or nacho chips

Nutrition:

Calories 761 kcal

Fat 28 g

Carbs 54 g

Protein 45 g

Barbacoa Beef

Basic Recipe

Preparation Time: 15 minutes

Cooking Time: 1hour and 20 minutes

Servings: 10

Ingredients:

1   2/3 cup beer

2   cloves garlic

3   chipotles in adobo sauce

4   1 tsp. black pepper

5   1/4 tsp. ground cloves

6   1 tbsp. olive oil

7   3-pound beef chuck roast, 2-inch chunks

8   bay leaves

9   1 onion, chopped

10 oz. chopped green chilies

11 1/4 cup lime juice

12 tbsp. apple cider vinegar

13 1 tbsp. ground cumin

14 1 tbsp. dried Mexican oregano

15 tsp. salt

Directions:

- Puree beer, garlic, chipotles, onion, green chilies, lime juice, vinegar, and seasonings.
- Sauté roast in oil.
- Add the bay leaves and pureed sauce.
- Cook on High Pressure for 60 minutes
- Discard the leaves.
- Shred beef and serve with sauce.

Nutrition:

Calories 520 kcal

Fat 23g

Carbs 56 g

Protein 31g

Maple Smoked Brisket

Basic Recipe

Preparation Time: 15 minutes

Cooking Time: 1hour and 20 minutes

Servings: 4

Ingredients:

- o lb. beef brisket
- tbsp. maple sugar
- c. bone broth or stock of choice
- 1 tbsp. liquid smoke
- fresh thyme sprigs
- tsp. smoked sea salt
- 1 tsp. black pepper
- 1 tsp. mustard powder
- 1 tsp. onion powder
- ½ tsp. smoked paprika

Directions:

1 Coat the brisket with all spices and sugar.

2 Sauté brisket in oil for 3 minutes

3 Add broth, liquid smoke, and thyme to the Air fryer and cover.

4 Cook at High Pressure for 50 minutes

5 Remove brisket.

6 Sauté sauce for 10 minutes

7   Serve sliced brisket with any whipped vegetable and
     sauce.

Nutrition:

Calories 1671 kcal

Fat 43g

Carbs 98 g

Protein 56g

Philly Cheesesteak Sandwiches

Basic Recipe

Preparation Time: 5 minutes

Cooking Time: 30 minutes

Servings: 8

Ingredients:

1. 3-pound beef top sirloin steak, sliced
2. onions, julienned
3. 1 can condensed French onion soup, undiluted
4. garlic cloves, minced
5. 1 package Italian salad dressing mix
6. tsp. beef base
7. 1/2 tsp. pepper
8. large red peppers, julienned

9 1/2 cup pickled pepper rings

10 hoagie buns, split

11 slices provolone cheese

Directions:

- Combine the first 7 ingredients in the pressure cooker. Adjust to pressure-cook on High for 10 minutes. Add peppers and pepper rings. Pressure-cook on High for 5 minutes

- Put beef, cheese, and vegetables on bun bottoms. Broil 1-2 minutes and serve.

Nutrition:

Calories 4852 kcal

Fat 67g

Carbs 360 g

Protein 86g

Pot Roast and Potatoes

Basic Recipe

Preparation Time: 15 minutes

Cooking Time: 1 hour and 15 minutes

Servings: 8

Ingredients:

1. tbsp. all-purpose flour
2. 1 tbsp. kosher salt
3. lb. chuck roast
4. 1 tbsp. black pepper
5. c. low-sodium beef broth
6. 1/2 c. red wine
7. 1 lb. baby potatoes, halved
8. 1 tbsp. Worcestershire sauce
9. carrots, sliced
10. 1 onion, chopped
11. 1 tbsp. extra-virgin olive oil
12. cloves garlic, minced
13. 1 tsp. thyme, chopped
14. tsp. rosemary, chopped
15. tbsp. tomato paste

Directions:

- Coat chuck roast with pepper and salt.
- Sauté the beef for 5 minutes on each side then set aside.
- Cook onion for 5 minutes

- Add herbs, garlic, and tomato paste and cook for 1 minute.
- Add four and wine and cook for 2 minutes
- Add Worcestershire sauce, broth, carrots, potatoes, salt and pepper.
- Put beef on top of the mixture
- High-Pressure Cook for an hour and serve.

Nutrition:

Calories 3274 kcal

Fat 42 g

Carbs 286 g

Protein 78 g

Butter Chicken

Intermediate Recipe

Preparation Time: 10 minutes

Cooking Time: 1hour and 10 minutes

Servings: 6

Ingredients:

1   1 tbsp. vegetable oil

2   1 tbsp. butter

3   1 onion, diced

4   tsp. grated ginger

5   1 tsp. ground cumin

6   1/2 tsp. turmeric

7   1/ 2 tsp. kosher salt

8   ½ tsp. black pepper

9   3/4 c. heavy cream

10   cloves garlic, chopped

11   oz. tomato paste

12   lb. boneless chicken thighs, 1" pieces

13   1 tbsp. garam masala

14   1 tsp. paprika

15   1 tbsp. sugar

Directions:

- Sauté the onion, ginger, and garlic in oil and butter
- Add tomato paste and cook for 3 minutes
- Add ½ cup water, chicken, and spices to the Pot.
- Pressure Cook on High for 5 minutes
- Add heavy cream.
- Serve with rice, naan, yogurt, and cilantro.

Nutrition:

Calories 3841

Fat 100g

Carbs 244g

Protein 150g

Curried Chicken Meatball Wraps

Basic Recipe

Preparation Time: 5 minutes

Cooking Time: 15 minutes

Servings: 12

Ingredients:

1   1 egg, beaten

2   1 onion, chopped

3   1/2 cup Rice Krispies

4   1/4 cup golden raisins

5   1/4 cup minced cilantro

6   tsp. curry powder

7   1/2 tsp. salt

8   Boston lettuce leaves

9   1 carrot, shredded

10 1/2 cup chopped salted peanuts

11 1-pound lean ground chicken

12 tbsp. olive oil

13 1 cup plain yogurt

Directions:

- Mix the first 7 ingredients.
- Shape mixture into 24 balls.
- Sauté meatballs on medium with oil
- Add water to pot.
- Put meatballs on the trivet in the pressure cooker.

- Pressure-cook on High for 7 minutes
- Mix yogurt and cilantro.
- Place 2 teaspoons sauce and 1 meatball in each lettuce leaf; top with remaining ingredients and serve.

Nutrition:

Calories 2525

Fat 80g

Carbs 225g

Protein 120g

Fall-Off-The-Bone Chicken

Intermediate Recipe

Preparation Time: 10 minutes

Cooking Time: 1hour and 10 minutes

Servings: 4

Ingredients:

1. 1 tbsp. packed brown sugar
2. 1 tbsp. chili powder
3. 1 tbsp. smoked paprika
4. 1 tsp. chopped thyme leaves
5. ¼ tbsp. kosher salt
6. ¼ tbsp. black pepper
7. 1 whole small chicken
8. 1 tbsp. extra-virgin olive oil
9. 2/3 c. low-sodium chicken broth
10. tbsp. chopped parsley

Directions:

- Coat chicken with brown sugar, chili powder, sugar, pepper, paprika, and thyme.
- Sauté chicken in oil for 3-4 minutes
- Pour broth in the Pot.
- Pressure Cook on High for 25 minutes
- Garnish sliced chicken with parsley and serve.

Nutrition:

Calories 1212

Fat 10g

Carbs 31g

Protein 15g

White Chicken Chili

Basic Recipe

Preparation Time: 5 minutes

Cooking Time: 30 minutes

Servings: 6

Ingredients:

1. 1 tbsp. vegetable oil
2. 1 red bell pepper, diced
   a. oz. condensed cream of chicken soup
3. tbsp. shredded Cheddar cheese
4. green onions, sliced
5. 1 cup Kernel corn
6. 1 tbsp. chili powder

7   oz. (2) boneless, skinless chicken breast

8   oz. white cannellini beans

9   1 cup Chunky Salsa

Directions:

- Sauté pepper, corn, and chili powder in oil for 2 minutes
- Season chicken with salt and pepper.
- Layer the beans, salsa, water, chicken, and soup over the corn mixture.
- Pressure Cook on High for 4 minutes
- Shred chicken and return to pot.
- Serve topped with cheese and green onions.

Nutrition:

Calories 1848

Fat 70g

Carbs 204g

Protein 90g

Coconut Curry Vegetable Rice Bowls

Basic Recipe

Preparation Time: 5 minutes

Cooking Time: 40minutes

Servings: 6

Ingredients:

1   2/3 cup uncooked brown rice
2   1 tsp. curry powder
3   3/4 tsp. salt divided
4   1 cup chopped green onion
5   1 cup sliced red bell pepper
6   1 tbsp. grated ginger
7   1 1/2 tbsp. sugar
8   1 cup matchstick carrots
9   1 cup chopped red cabbage
10 oz. sliced water chestnuts
11 oz. no salt added chickpeas
12 oz. coconut milk

Directions:

- Add rice, water, curry powder, and 1/4 tsp. of the salt in the Air fryer. Pressure Cook for 15 minutes. Sauté for 2 minutes and serve.

Nutrition:

Calories 1530

Fat 110g

Carbs 250g

Protein 80g

Egg Roll in a Bowl

Basic Recipe

Preparation Time: 5 minutes

Cooking Time: 20 minutes

Servings: 4

Ingredients:

1. 1/3 cup low-sodium soy sauce
2. tbsp. sesame oil
3. 1 cup matchstick cut carrots
4. 1 bunch green onions, sliced
5. bags coleslaw mix
6. 1 lb. ground chicken
7. tbsp. sesame seeds
8. cloves garlic, minced
9. oz. shiitake mushrooms, sliced
10. 1 1/2 cups chicken broth

Directions:

- Add sesame oil, ground chicken, soy sauce, garlic, chicken broth and mushrooms to Air fryer.
- Cook for 2 minutes on High Pressure.
- Add in coleslaw mix and carrots.
- Let sit for 5 minutes
- Serve with sesame seeds and green onions.

Nutrition:

Calories 3451

Fat 130g

Carbs 301g

Protein 150g

Frittata Provencal

Basic Recipe

Preparation Time: 5 minutes

Cooking Time: 45 minutes

Servings: 6

Ingredients:

1   eggs

2   1 tsp. minced thyme

3   1 tsp. hot pepper sauce

4   1/2 tsp. salt

5   1/4 tsp. pepper

6   oz. goat cheese, divided

7   1/2 cup chopped sun-dried tomatoes

8   1 tbsp. olive oil

9   1 potato, peeled and sliced

10 1 onion, sliced

11 1/2 tsp. smoked paprika

Directions:

- Sauté potato, paprika, and onion in oil for 5-7 minutes

- Transfer potato mixture to a greased baking dish.

- Pour the first 6 ingredients over potato mixture.

- Cover baking dish with foil.

- Add water and trivet to pot.

- Use a foil sling to lower the dish onto the trivet.

- Adjust to pressure-cook on high for 35 minutes and serve.

Nutrition:

Calories 2554

Fat 70g

Carbs 190g

Protein 80g

Ramekin Eggs

Basic Recipe

Preparation Time: 2 minutes

Cooking Time: 3minutes

Servings: 2

Ingredients:

1   1 tbsp. ghee, plus more for greasing

2   cups mushrooms, chopped

3   ¼ tsp. salt

4   1 tbsp. chives, chopped

5   eggs

6   tbsp. heavy cream

Directions:

- Sauté mushrooms with ghee and salt until tender.
- Put mushrooms into greased ramekins.
- Add chives, egg, and cream.
- Add water, trivet, and ramekins to pot.
- Pressure Cook on Low for 1-2 minutes
- Serve with freshly toasted bread.

Nutrition:

Calories 703

Fat 5g

Carbs 20g

Protein 7g

Easter Ham

Basic Recipe

Preparation Time: 5 minutes

Cooking Time: 15 minutes

Servings: 8

Ingredients:

1 1/2 c. orange marmalade

2 ¼ tsp. black pepper

3 1 (4-6 lb.) fully cooked, spiral, bone-in ham

4 1/4 c. brown sugar

5 1/4 c. orange juice

6 tbsp. Dijon mustard

Directions:

- Mix marmalade, brown sugar, orange juice, Dijon, and black pepper.
- Coat ham with glaze.
- Cook on Meat for 15 minutes
- Serve ham with more glaze from the Pot.

Nutrition:

Calories 3877

Fat 80g

Carbs 207g

Protein 100g

Korean Lamb Chops

Intermediate Recipe

Preparation Time: 10 minutes

Cooking Time: 50minutes

Servings: 6

Ingredients:

1. lbs. Lamb chops
2. 1/2 tsp. Red pepper powder
3. tbsp. granulated sugar
4. 1 tbsp. curry powder
5. 1/2 tbsp. soy sauce
6. tbsp. rice wine
7. tbsp. garlic, minced
8. 1 tsp. ginger, minced
9. bay leaves
10. 1 cup carrots, diced
11. cups onions, diced
12. 1 cup celery, diced
13. tbsp. Korean red pepper paste
14. tbsp. ketchup
15. tbsp. Corn syrup
16. 1/2 tbsp. sesame oil
17. 1/2 tsp. cinnamon powder
18. 1 tsp. sesame seeds

19 1 tsp. black pepper

20 1/3 cup Asian pear ground

21 1/3 cup onion powder

22 1/2 tbsp. Green plum extract

23 1 cup red wine

Directions:

- Put all ingredients except cilantro and green onions into the Air fryer.
- Pressure Cook for 20 minutes
- Sauté until sauce is thickened.
- Add water and lamb on trivet to pot.
- Broil at 400°F for 5 minutes
- Serve with chopped cilantro and green onions.

Nutrition:

Calories 2728

Fat 220g

Carbs 551g

Protein 250g

Air Fryer Chicken Kabobs

Basic Recipe

Preparation Time: 15 minutes

Cooking Time: 15 minutes

Servings: 2

Ingredients:

1   Chicken breasts, chopped

2   Mushrooms cut into halves

3   ⅓ Cup honey

4   ⅓ Cup Soy sauce -

5   1 teaspoon Pepper, crushed

6   1 teaspoon Sesame seeds

7   Bell peppers, in different colors

8   Cooking oil spray as required

Directions:

- Cut the chicken breasts into small cubes, wash and pat dry. Rub little pepper and salt over the chicken. Sprits some oil on it. In a small bowl, combine honey and soy sauce thoroughly.

- Add the sesame seeds into the mix. Drive in chicken, bell peppers and mushrooms onto the skewers.

- Set the air fryer at 170 degrees Celsius and preheat.

- Drizzle with the kabobs with the honey and soy sauce mixture.

- Put all the skewed chicken kabobs into the air fryer basket and cook for 20 minutes

- Rotate the skewer intermittently in between.

- Serve hot.

Nutrition:

Calories 392

Fat 5g

Carbs 65.4g

Protein 6.7g

Chicken Fried Rice in Air Fryer

Basic Recipe

Preparation Time: 20 minutes

Cooking Time: 20 minutes

Servings: 4

Ingredients:

1. cups cooked cold white rice
2. 1 cup chicken cooked & diced
3. 1 cup carrots and peas, frozen
4. 1 tablespoon vegetable oil
5. 1 tablespoon soy sauce
6. ½ cup onion
7. ¼ teaspoon salt

Directions:

- In a large bowl, put the cooked cold rice.
- Stir in soy sauce and vegetable oil.
- Now add the frozen carrots and peas, diced chicken, diced onion, salt and combine.
- Transfer the rice mixture into the mix.
- Take a non-stick pan which you can comfortably place in the air fryer and transfer the complete rice mixture into the pan.
- Place the pan in the air fryer.

- Set the temperature at 180 degree Celsius and timer for 20 minutes
- Remove the pan after the set time elapse.
- Serve hot.

Nutrition:

Calories 618

Fat 5.5g

Carbs 116.5g

Protein 21.5g

Air Fried Chicken Tikkas

Basic Recipe

Preparation Time: 10 minutes

Cooking Time: 15 minutes

Servings: 4

Ingredients:

For marinade:

1. 1¼ pounds chicken, bones cut into small bite size
2. ¼ pound cherry tomatoes
3. 1 cup yogurt
4. 1 tablespoon ginger garlic paste (fresh)
5. bell peppers, 1" cut size
6. tablespoons chili powder
7. tablespoons cumin powder
8. 1 tablespoon turmeric powder
9. tablespoons coriander powder
10. 1 teaspoon garam masala powder
11. teaspoons olive oil
12. Salt: to taste

For garnishing:

- 1 lemon, cut into half
- ⅓ cup Coriander, fresh, chopped
- 1 medium Onion, nicely sliced
- Mint leaves, fresh: few

1. **Directions:**
2. In a large bowl mix all the marinade ingredients and coat it thoroughly on the chicken pieces.
3. Cover the bowl and set aside for 2 hours minimum. If you can refrigerate overnight, it can give better marinade effect.
4. Thread the chicken in the skewers along with bell peppers and tomatoes alternately.
5. Preheat your air fryer at 200 degrees Celsius.
6. Spread an aluminum liner on the air fryer basket and arrange the skewers on it.
7. Set the timer for 15 minutes and grill it.
8. Turn the skewer intermittently for an even grilling.
9. Once done, put into a plate and garnish with the given ingredients before serving.

Nutrition:

Calories 400

Fat 20g

Carbs 17.4g

Protein 46.9g

Nashville Hot Chicken in Air Fryer

Basic Recipe

Preparation Time: 10 minutes

Cooking Time: 27 minutes

Servings: 4

Ingredients:

- pounds chicken with bones, 8 pieces
- tablespoons vegetable oil
- cups all-purpose flour
- 1 cup buttermilk
- tablespoons paprika
- 1 teaspoon onion powder
- 1 teaspoon garlic powder
- 1 teaspoon ground black pepper
- teaspoons salt

For Hot sauce:

1. 1 tablespoon cayenne pepper
2. ¼ cup vegetable oil
3. 1 teaspoon salt
4. slices white bread
5. Dill pickle, as required

Directions:

- Clean and wash chicken thoroughly, pat dry and keep ready aside.

- In a bowl, whisk buttermilk and eggs.
- Combine garlic powder, black pepper, paprika, onion powder, All-purpose flour and salt in a bowl.
- Now dip the chicken in the egg and buttermilk and put in the second bowl marinade bowl and toss to get an even coating. Maybe you need to repeat the process twice for a better coat.
- After that spray some vegetable oil and keep aside.
- Before cooking the chicken, pre-heat the fryer at 190 degrees Celsius.
- Brush vegetable oil on the fry basket before start cooking.
- Now place the coated chicken in the air fryer at 190 degrees Celsius and set the timer for 20 minutes. Do not crowd the air fryer. It would be better if you can do the frying in 2 batches.
- Keep the flipping the chicken intermittently for even frying.
- Once the set timer elapsed, remove the chicken to a plate and keep it there without covering.
- Now start the second batch. Do the same process.
- After 20 minutes, reduce the temperature to 170 degrees Celsius and place the first batch of chicken over the second batch, which is already in the air fry basket.
- Fry it again for another 7 minutes
- While the chicken is air frying, make the hot sauce.

- In a bowl mix salt and cayenne pepper thoroughly.
- In a small saucepan, heat some vegetable oil.
- When the oil becomes hot add the spice mix and continue stirring to become smooth.
- While serving, place the chicken over the white bread and spread the hot sauce over the chicken.
- Use dill pickle to top it.
- Serve hot.

Nutrition:

Calories 1013

Fat 22.2g

Carbs 53.9g

Protein 140.7g

Air Fryer Panko Breaded Chicken Parmesan

Basic Recipe

Preparation Time: 10 minutes

Cooking Time: 20 minutes

Servings: 4

Ingredients:

1. ounces chicken breasts, skinless
2. 1 cup panko bread crumbs
3. ⅛ cup egg whites
4. ½ cup parmesan cheese, shredded
5. ½ cup mozzarella cheese, grated
6. ¾ cup marinara sauce
7. ½ teaspoon salt
8. 1 teaspoon ground pepper
9. teaspoons italian seasoning
10. Cooking spray, as required

Directions:

- Cut each chicken breast into halves to make 4 breast pieces. Wash and pat dry.
- Place the chicken in a chopping board and pound to flatten.
- Sprits the air fryer basket with cooking oil.
- Set the temperature of air fryer to 200 degrees Celsius and preheat.

- In a large bowl, mix cheese, panko breadcrumbs, and seasoning ingredients.
- Put the egg white in a large bowl.
- Dip the pounded chicken into the egg whites and dredge into breadcrumb mixture.
- Now place the coated chicken into the air fryer basket and spray some cooking oil.
- Start cooking the chicken breasts for 7 minutes
- Dress on top of the chicken breasts with shredded mozzarella and marinara sauce.
- Continue cooking for another 3 minutes and remove for serving when the cheese starts to melt.

Nutrition:

Calories 347

Fat 15g

Carbs 7.4g

Protein 37g

30-Day Meal Plan

Day	Breakfast	Lunch/dinner	Dessert
1	Shrimp Skillet	Spinach Rolls	Matcha Crepe Cake
2	Coconut Yogurt with Chia Seeds	Goat Cheese Fold-Overs	Pumpkin Spices Mini Pies
3	Chia Pudding	Crepe Pie	Nut Bars
4	Egg Fat Bombs	Coconut Soup	Pound Cake
5	Morning "Grits"	Fish Tacos	Tortilla Chips with Cinnamon Recipe
6	Scotch Eggs	Cobb Salad	Granola Yogurt with Berries
7	Bacon Sandwich	Cheese Soup	Berry Sorbet
8	Noatmeal	Tuna Tartare	Coconut Berry Smoothie
9	Breakfast Bake with Meat	Clam Chowder	Coconut Milk Banana Smoothie

10	Breakfast Bagel	Asian Beef Salad	Mango Pineapple Smoothie
11	Egg and Vegetable Hash	Keto Carbonara	Raspberry Green Smoothie
12	Cowboy Skillet	Cauliflower Soup with Seeds	Loaded Berries Smoothie
13	Feta Quiche	Prosciutto-Wrapped Asparagus	Papaya Banana and Kale Smoothie
14	Bacon Pancakes	Stuffed Bell Peppers	Green Orange Smoothie
15	Waffles	Stuffed Eggplants with Goat Cheese	Double Berries Smoothie
16	Chocolate Shake	Korma Curry	Energizing Protein Bars
17	Eggs in Portobello Mushroom Hats	Zucchini Bars	Sweet and Nutty Brownies
18	Matcha Fat Bombs	Mushroom Soup	Keto Macho Nachos

19	Keto Smoothie Bowl	Stuffed Portobello Mushrooms	Peanut Butter Choco Banana Gelato with Mint
20	Salmon Omelet	Lettuce Salad	Cinnamon Peaches and Yogurt
21	Hash Brown	Onion Soup	Pear Mint Honey Popsicles
22	Black's Bangin' Casserole	Asparagus Salad	Orange and Peaches Smoothie
23	Bacon Cups	Cauliflower Tabbouleh	Coconut Spiced Apple Smoothie
24	Spinach Eggs and Cheese	Beef Salpicao	Sweet and Nutty Smoothie
25	Taco Wraps	Stuffed Artichoke	Ginger Berry Smoothie
26	Coffee Donuts	Spinach Rolls	Vegetarian Friendly Smoothie
27	Egg Baked Omelet	Goat Cheese Fold-Overs	ChocNut Smoothie
28	Ranch Risotto	Crepe Pie	Coco Strawberry Smoothie

29	Scotch Eggs	Coconut Soup	Egg Spinach Berries Smoothie
30	Fried Eggs	Fish Tacos	Creamy Dessert Smoothie

Conclusion

Thanks for making it to the end of this book. An air fryer is a relatively new addition to the kitchen, and it's easy to see why people are getting excited about using it. With an air fryer, you can make crispy fries, chicken wings, chicken breasts and steaks in minutes. There are many delicious foods that you can prepare without adding oil or grease to your meal. Again make sure to read the instructions on your air fryer and follow the rules for proper usage and maintenance. Once your air fryer is in good working condition, you can really get creative and start experimenting your way to healthy food that tastes great.

That's it! Thank you!

CPSIA information can be obtained
at www.ICGtesting.com
Printed in the USA
BVHW052032120421
604748BV00001B/37